I0459357

FROM PAYCHECK TO POWER

Simple Ways to Make, Save, and Protect Your Money

ABOUT THE AUTHOR

LaToya Hunter is a financial educator and banking professional with over a decade of experience helping individuals and families better understand their money.

Through years of hands-on work in the financial industry, she has seen firsthand how lack of education—not lack of income—keeps many people stuck in cycles of stress and uncertainty. Her passion is helping everyday people build confidence, clarity, and practical systems that allow their money to support the life they want to live.

In From Paycheck to Power, LaToya shares the lessons, habits, and mindset shifts she has learned through both professional experience and real life. Her approach is honest, practical, and judgment-free—focused on progress, not perfection.

When she is not teaching or coaching, LaToya Hunter enjoys spending time with her family, traveling and continuing to learn new ways to empower others through financial education.

"I didn't wake up one day with savings, businesses, or multiple streams of income.

I learned money the long way. With small steps, mistakes, discipline, and systems that actually worked.

I'm not a financial expert.
I'm not a Wall Street anything.

I'm simply someone who grew up without much, taught myself how money really works, and decided to stop hoping my card would go through and start deciding where my money goes."

HOW TO USE THIS BOOK

This book is designed to meet you where you are — not where you think you "should" be.

You don't need to read it straight through.
You don't need to do everything at once.
And you don't need to be perfect.

Each chapter is meant to be practical, approachable, and realistic. Some chapters will ask you to reflect. Others will guide you to take small, intentional action. You may find that certain sections speak to you more than others, depending on the season you're in — that's okay.

Here's how to get the most out of this book:

- Read at your own pace. One chapter at a time is enough.
- Use the exercises honestly, not ideally. Progress matters more than perfection.
- Revisit chapters as needed. Your financial life will change, and this book can grow with you.
- Focus on consistency, not comparison. Your journey does not need to look like anyone else's.

This book isn't about doing everything "right."
It's about building awareness, confidence, and systems that support your real life.

Take what you need.

Leave what you don't.

And remember — small steps add up.

TABLE OF CONTENTS

SECTION I: THE FOUNDATION
Understanding Your Relationship with Money

SECTION II: BUILDING STABILITY
Creating Systems That Support You

SECTION III: GROWTH & CREDIT
Using Financial Tools Wisely

SECTION IV: SUSTAINING THE JOURNEY
Confidence, Consistency, and Practice

CHAPTER 1
MY MONEY STORY, WHERE I COME FROM MATTERS

Learning Money the Long Way

I didn't wake up one day and suddenly have savings, businesses, or extra streams of income.

My journey looked more like this:

- Trying to save money in traditional savings accounts
- Learning how to discipline myself with small amounts
- Slowly building credit and understanding the game
- Making mistakes, fixing them, and learning from everyone
- Teaching myself how money actually works

Little by little, things started to shift.

I became a homeowner at 35 — something younger me didn't even realize was possible.

I bought brand-new cars, not because of luck, but because I finally had systems in place that protected my money instead of leaking it.

I started multiple businesses, including one in the travel industry — something that allowed me to create multiple streams of income while actually seeing the world.

MONEY CHECK

Answer honestly — no judgment.

- What was money like in the home you grew up in?

- What beliefs about money are you ready to release?

- What habit do you want to build next?

REAL TALK

I didn't grow up learning how money worked.

I wasn't taught about saving, credit, or building wealth early on.
What I learned instead was how to get by, how to stretch, and how to make things work with what I had.

For a long time, I thought money success was about income alone.
If I could just make more, everything would fall into place.
What I didn't realize was that without understanding money, more income would only create bigger problems.

My relationship with money was shaped by what I saw, what I didn't have, and what no one ever explained to me.
That mattered more than I knew at the time.

Once I started paying attention to where I came from financially,
I could finally understand why certain habits were hard to break
and why mindset had to change before anything else could.

KEY TAKEAWAYS

 You don't need to be rich to start.

 You need intention.

 You need structure.

 You need consistency.

POWER MOVE

Choose ONE action from this chapter and complete it this week. Write it below with the steps needed to ensure this action is truly completed.

_____

_____

_____

_____

_____

_____

_____

_____

SMALL STEPS CREATE MOMENTUM.

CHAPTER 1A

YOUR MINDSET MATTERS MORE THAN YOUR SALARY BECAUSE YOU CAN'T OUT-EARN BAD MONEY HABITS

Your relationship with money matters more than your income.

⊘ Not your job title.

⊘ Not your credit score.

⊘ Not how much you make.

Your mindset.

After over a decade in banking, I learned this truth firsthand:
Your mindset determines your money more than your paycheck ever will.

Scarcity vs Growth Mindset

Scarcity mindset sounds like:

- "I'll never get ahead."
- "Saving is impossible for me."
- "Money stresses me out."

Growth mindset sounds like:

- "I can learn better habits."
- "Small steps matter."
- "My financial life can change."

REAL TALK

 **Avoidance is expensive.**

 **Awareness is empowering.**

For a long time, I believed the problem was my income.

I thought if I could just make more money, everything would finally feel easier. But what I learned the hard way is that more money doesn't fix confusion — it exposes it.

I watched people who made less than I did manage their money better, and people who made more still live paycheck to paycheck.
That's when it clicked: salary isn't the deciding factor — mindset is.

Until I learned how money actually works, how to prioritize it, protect it, and plan with intention, my income didn't matter as much as I thought it did.

Once my mindset shifted, my decisions shifted. And once my decisions shifted, the numbers finally started to make sense.

MONEY RESET

One money belief I want to release:

_____

One money belief I want to embrace:

_____

CHAPTER 2
TAKING INVENTORY
UNDERSTANDING YOUR
CURRENT FINANCIAL REALITY

Before We Talk Strategy, We Need Truth!

Before we talk about saving, budgeting, or making more money, we have to start with something simple — but powerful:

Knowing exactly where you stand.

- Not where you wish you were.
- Not where you think you are.
- But where you actually are.

This chapter is about awareness — because you can't fix what you won't face.

Why Most People Avoid Their Finances

Most people don't avoid their money because they're irresponsible.

They avoid it because it feels overwhelming, emotional, or embarrassing.

People avoid their finances because:
- They're afraid of what they'll see
- They don't know where to start
- They feel behind
- They've made mistakes before

Avoidance doesn't make problems disappear. It makes them louder.

REAL TALK

 Avoidance is expensive.

 Awareness is empowering.

Taking inventory was uncomfortable for me at first.

I avoided looking too closely at my accounts because I already knew things weren't where I wanted them to be. I told myself I would deal with it "later," but later never came until I made the decision to face the numbers head-on.

What surprised me most wasn't how bad things were — it was how much clarity I gained once I actually looked. Seeing everything in one place helped me understand my habits, my patterns, and the choices I was making without even realizing it.

Taking inventory didn't shame me.
It empowered me.

Once I knew where my money was going, I could finally decide where I wanted it to go instead.

What "Taking Inventory" Really Means

Taking inventory isn't about perfection.
It's about clarity.

It means gathering the facts about your money so you can build a plan that actually works.

This is information — not a verdict.

What You'll Need to Take Inventory
You don't need anything fancy. You just need honesty and about 30 minutes.

Gather:

- Your most recent bank statements
- Credit card statements
- Your last pay stub
- A notebook, spreadsheet, or notes app

No apps required.
No judgment allowed.

KEY TAKEAWAY

 **You cannot build a plan on guesses.**

▷▷ **Clarity is the foundation of financial power.**

MONEY CHECK

Answer honestly.

How much money comes in each month?

_____

What bills must be paid no matter what?

_____

What expenses surprise you regularly?

_____

What debt causes the most stress?

_____

What number have you been avoiding?

_____

POWER MOVE

This week, complete a full financial inventory.

No fixing.
No changing.
Just awareness.

You can't move forward until you know where you're standing.

Journal what you learned below to hold yourself accountable to this power move.

_____

_____

_____

_____

_____

_____

_____

_____

_____

CHAPTER 3
AUTOMATIONS THAT SAVE YOU EVEN WHEN YOU FORGET

Why Income Growth Matters

Saving alone can only take you so far.
At some point, increasing income creates flexibility, breathing room, and options.

Multiple streams don't mean working nonstop.
They mean being intentional about how money flows into your life.

What Automation Really Means

Automation is simply money moving automatically from checking to savings.

You decide:
- The amount
- The timing
- The frequency

After that, the system works for you.

REAL TALK

➤ Motivation is unreliable.

➤ Systems are not.

For a long time, I tried to save money the traditional way — by manually moving it when I remembered or waiting to see what was "left over." The problem was, there was rarely anything left.

What finally changed things for me was automation.

Once I understood savings automation, it made saving consistent and effortless, and showed me there are multiple ways and types of accounts to save and protect money based on different financial goals. I realized I didn't need more motivation—I needed a system.

REAL TALK (CONT'D)

✓ Automating even small amounts made a difference.

✓ Money started moving before I could spend it.

✓ Saving became consistent instead of occasional.

The biggest lesson for me was this: relying on willpower will always fail eventually. Systems don't.

Once I stopped depending on myself to remember and started letting automation do the work, saving finally became sustainable.

KEY TAKEAWAY

- If saving is optional, life will take the money first.

POWER MOVE

- Set up one automatic transfer this week — even if it's small.

WRITE IT OUT

- What parts of my financial life feel hardest to manage consistently, and why?
- If I didn't have to rely on motivation or willpower, what systems or automations could support me instead?
- What is one small automated change I could make that would reduce stress
- and help me stay consistent?

_____

_____

_____

_____

Consistency matters more than amount.

CHAPTER 4
SAVINGS CHALLENGES THAT ACTUALLY WORK

Saving money often feels harder than it should.

Many people try to save by relying on willpower alone — putting money aside only when there is something left over. The problem with this approach is that "leftover money" rarely exists.

Savings works best when it feels achievable, flexible, and aligned with real life. Small, consistent actions create momentum far more effectively than large, unrealistic goals.

Why Traditional Saving Often Fails

Traditional savings advice usually focuses on saving large amounts quickly or cutting spending drastically. While this may work short-term, it often leads to burnout or frustration.

Why High-Yield Savings Accounts Work:

A high-yield savings account is an account that pays more interest than a traditional bank account, helping your money grow faster while staying safe and accessible. When I started using one, I realized my money could finally work for me.

Savings challenges work because they:
- Start small
- Build consistency
- Create visible progress
- Feel manageable rather than restrictive

The goal is not perfection — it's progress.

Examples of Savings Challenges That Work

Savings challenges can look different depending on your lifestyle and income. The key is choosing a challenge that feels realistic for you.

Some effective approaches include:
- Saving small, increasing amounts over time
- No-spend days or weekends
- Automatically saving small bills or round-ups
- Designating specific savings goals instead of one general account

The best challenge is the one you can stick with.

REAL TALK

I used to think saving only worked if I could put away large amounts at once.
If I couldn't save "enough," I wouldn't save anything at all.

That mindset kept me stuck.

What finally worked for me was starting small and staying consistent.
Instead of trying to save hundreds of dollars at a time, I focused on manageable amounts — the kind that didn't disrupt my life or make me feel deprived.

I experimented with different saving methods until I found what fit.
Sometimes that meant setting aside small weekly amounts.
Other times it meant saving extra money I wasn't expecting.

The point wasn't the method — it was building the habit.

Saving stopped feeling overwhelming once I realized it didn't have to be perfect.
Progress added up faster than I expected, simply because I stayed committed instead of giving up when things weren't ideal.

POWER MOVE

Choose one savings challenge that feels realistic for you right now.
Write down:
- The challenge you are choosing   _____
- How much you will save   _____
- How long you will commit to it   _____

Commit to this challenge for the next 30 days.

JOURNAL

What has made saving money difficult for me in the past?

Which type of savings challenge feels most realistic for my current lifestyle, and why?

How could starting smaller help me stay consistent instead of giving up?

_____

_____

_____

_____

_____

_____

_____

_____

_____

CHAPTER 5
PROTECTING YOUR MONEY: THE OVERLOOKED STEPS

Saving money is important, but protecting the money you already have is just as critical.

Many people focus on earning more or saving more, yet overlook the small gaps where money quietly slips away. These leaks often don't feel dramatic, but over time they can undo a lot of hard work.

What "Protecting Your Money" Really Means

Protecting your money doesn't require fear or extreme caution.
It simply means paying attention.

Protection looks like:
- Knowing where your money is
- Monitoring accounts regularly
- Understanding who has access
- Being aware of common scams and errors

When you protect your money, you create stability and peace of mind.

Common Ways Money Gets Lost

Money is often lost not through major mistakes, but through small oversights.

These can include:
- Forgotten subscriptions
- Incorrect charges
- Missed alerts or notifications
- Unmonitored accounts
- Outdated account information

Awareness is one of the most powerful financial tools you have.

REAL TALK

I used to think protecting my money meant simply not spending it.
What I didn't understand was how much money could be lost just by not paying attention.

Protecting my money started with awareness and simple actions, not complicated strategies.

Some of the most impactful changes I made were:
* Adding beneficiaries to my accounts so my money was properly protected
* Reviewing my accounts regularly instead of assuming everything was fine
* Identifying subscriptions and recurring charges I no longer needed
* Catching incorrect or unfamiliar charges early instead of after the fact

Once I made these things part of my routine, I noticed fewer surprises and less stress around my finances.

Protecting my money didn't require perfection.

It required consistency, attention, and the willingness to check in regularly.

POWER MOVE

Choose one financial account today and review it carefully.

Check for:
• Recent transactions
• Subscriptions or recurring charges
• Checking and updating beneficiaries on all accounts.

Write down one adjustment you can make to better protect your money.

JOURNAL

Where might money be leaking out of my life without my full awareness?

What financial habits or accounts do I avoid checking — and why?

How would paying closer attention change how secure I feel about my money?

_____

_____

_____

_____

_____

_____

_____

_____

_____

CHAPTER 6
CREATING NEW INCOME: MULTIPLE STREAMS THAT ACTUALLY WORK

Saving and budgeting are powerful, but there is a limit to how much you can cut.

At some point, growing your income becomes part of the conversation. Additional income creates breathing room, flexibility, and opportunity — especially when life changes or unexpected expenses arise.

What "Multiple Streams" Really Means

Multiple streams of income do not mean working nonstop or juggling ten jobs. They mean being intentional about how money flows into your life.

A stream of income can be:
- Overtime or bonuses
- Freelance or contract work
- A side business
- Skill-based services
- Income from something you already know how to do

The goal is sustainability, not exhaustion.

Why Starting Small Matters

Many people delay creating additional income because they believe they need everything figured out first. In reality, most income streams grow through experimentation, learning, and adjustment.

Starting small allows you to:
- Build confidence
- Learn what works for you
- Avoid unnecessary risk
- Grow at a pace that fits your life

Progress happens one step at a time.

REAL TALK

For a long time, I thought creating more income meant doing something completely new or taking big risks. I didn't realize that additional income often starts with what you already know.

My first shifts didn't come from some perfect business plan. They came from recognizing skills and opportunities that were already in front of me and being willing to explore them without overcomplicating the process.

What made the biggest difference was changing how I thought about income:
- I stopped waiting for the "right time" to start
- I focused on one additional stream at a time instead of trying to do everything
- I allowed income streams to grow gradually instead of expecting instant results
- I learned through trial, adjustment, and experience — not perfection

Creating multiple streams wasn't about working nonstop.

It was about building flexibility and giving myself options.

Once I stopped seeing income growth as overwhelming and started seeing it as intentional, it became much more realistic — and sustainable.

POWER MOVE

List three skills or experiences you already have.
Circle one that feels realistic to explore as an income opportunity.

_____

_____

_____

Write down one small action you could take this week to begin exploring that option.

_____

JOURNAL

What fears or assumptions have held me back from exploring additional income?

What would "starting small" look like for me right now?

_____

_____

_____

_____

_____

_____

_____

_____

_____

_____

CHAPTER 7

BUDGETING BASICS FOR REAL LIFE: HOW TO TELL YOUR MONEY WHERE TO GO

Budgeting often gets a bad reputation.

Many people think a budget means restriction, punishment, or constantly telling yourself "no." In reality, a budget is simply a plan for your money — one that allows you to decide where it goes instead of wondering where it went.

A realistic budget reflects your actual life, not an ideal version of it.

What Budgeting Is — and Isn't

A budget is not about perfection.
It's not about tracking every dollar obsessively.
And it's not about comparison.

Budgeting is about awareness, intention, and alignment.

When your money has direction, decisions become easier, and stress decreases.

Simple Budget Categories That Work

Budgets don't need to be complicated to be effective.

Most budgets work best when they include a few clear categories:

- Fixed expenses
- Variable expenses
- Savings
- Lifestyle or flexible spending

The goal is not to eliminate enjoyment, but to create balance.

REAL TALK

For a long time, budgeting felt overwhelming to me because I thought it had to be perfect. I tried tracking every dollar, every receipt, and every expense — and I would eventually quit because it felt unrealistic.

What finally worked was simplifying the process.

Instead of overcomplicating things, I focused on understanding my main categories and where my money was consistently going. Once I saw patterns in my spending, I could make adjustments without feeling restricted or guilty.

Budgeting became less about control and more about clarity.
Once I gave my money direction, I stopped feeling surprised by my finances and started feeling more confident in my decisions.

MONEY CHECK

Look at your last month of spending.

Which category surprised you the most?

_____

Which category needs clearer limits?

_____

Which category deserves more flexibility?

_____

Write down one adjustment you can make next month.

_____

CHAPTER 8
EMERGENCY FUNDS:
YOUR FINANCIAL SEATBELT

Life doesn't wait until your finances are perfect to happen.

Unexpected expenses show up without warning — car repairs, medical bills, job changes, or emergencies you didn't plan for. An emergency fund exists to protect you when life happens, not to restrict you when things are going well.

An emergency fund gives you options.

What an Emergency Fund Really Does

Emergency funds are not about fear.
They are about protection and peace of mind.

When you have money set aside for the unexpected:
- You rely less on credit
- You avoid panic decisions
- You maintain control during stressful moments

An emergency fund is a buffer between you and financial chaos.

How Much Is Enough?

Emergency funds don't have to be built all at once.

Starting with a small, realistic goal creates momentum. Many people begin with one month of essential expenses and gradually work toward a larger cushion over time.

The most important part is starting — not finishing.

REAL TALK

For a long time, I didn't prioritize an emergency fund because I didn't think I could afford to. I told myself I would start saving once everything else was handled — and that moment never came.

What I learned was that emergencies don't wait for perfect timing. Without a buffer, even small issues felt overwhelming and stressful.

Once I started building an emergency fund, even in small amounts, things felt different. I wasn't panicking every time something unexpected came up. I had options, and that alone changed how I approached my finances.

The peace of mind mattered just as much as the money itself.

POWER MOVE

Set a starter emergency fund goal.

Write down:

- The amount you want to start with _____
- Where the money will be saved   _____
- How you will contribute to it   _____

Even small, consistent contributions make a difference.

JOURNAL

How do I usually respond when unexpected expenses come up?

What emotions come up for me when I think about emergencies and money?

How would having an emergency fund change how I feel during stressful moments?

_____

_____

_____

_____

_____

_____

_____

_____

_____

CHAPTER 9
SINKING FUNDS:
THE SECRET TO STRESS-FREE
SPENDING

Sinking funds are one of the most overlooked tools in personal finance.

They help you prepare for expenses you already know are coming, instead of reacting to them when they arrive. Sinking funds turn predictable costs into planned spending.

Why Sinking Funds Matter

Many expenses feel like emergencies simply because they weren't planned for. Things like car maintenance, holidays, travel, or medical costs are not surprises — they're expected.

Sinking funds allow you to spread the cost of these expenses over time, reducing stress and avoiding last-minute financial strain.

Common Sinking Fund Categories

Sinking funds can be created for almost anything.

Some common examples include:
- Car maintenance
- Holidays and gifts
- Travel and vacations
- Medical or health expenses
- School activities or family events

The categories should reflect your real life, not an ideal one.

REAL TALK

Before I understood sinking funds, expenses felt like they came out of nowhere — even when I knew they were coming. A car repair or a holiday would show up and immediately throw everything off.

Once I started using sinking funds, things changed.
Instead of scrambling or stressing, I already had money set aside for those moments.

Saving a little at a time felt far more manageable than trying to cover the full cost all at once. It also helped me stop using credit for expenses that were completely predictable.

Sinking funds gave me peace of mind.
They allowed me to enjoy things like travel or celebrations without guilt or financial stress.

POWER MOVE

Choose one upcoming expense that usually causes stress.
Create a sinking fund for it.

Write down:
- The expense
- The total amount needed
- How much you can set aside regularly

Start with what feels realistic.

JOURNAL

What expenses tend to stress me out the most each year?

Which of those expenses could be planned for instead of treated as emergencies?

How would sinking funds change the way I experience those moments?

_____

_____

_____

_____

_____

_____

_____

_____

_____

CHAPTER 10

CREDIT: BUILDING, PROTECTING, AND USING IT WISELY

Credit is often misunderstood.

Many people are taught to fear credit or avoid it altogether, while others are encouraged to use it without fully understanding how it works. In reality, credit is simply a tool — one that can either support your financial goals or create unnecessary stress, depending on how it's used.

What Credit Really Represents

Credit reflects patterns and behavior over time.

It is influenced by things like:
- Payment history
- Credit utilization
- Length of credit history
- Account management

Understanding credit allows you to make informed decisions instead of reactive ones.

Healthy Credit Habits

Building and maintaining healthy credit doesn't require perfection.
It requires consistency.

Some foundational habits include:
- Paying bills on time
- Keeping balances manageable
- Monitoring accounts regularly
- Using credit intentionally instead of emotionally

REAL TALK

For a long time, I avoided credit because I didn't fully understand it. I either ignored it or felt anxious every time I thought about it, which didn't help my situation at all.

Once I took the time to learn how credit actually worked, things shifted. I realized that credit wasn't the problem — my lack of understanding was.

As I became more intentional, I started paying closer attention to balances, due dates, and how often I was using credit. Small changes made a noticeable difference over time.

Credit stopped feeling intimidating once I learned how to use it as a tool instead of letting it control my decisions.

One of the major shifts that changed everything for me was starting to review my credit report annually.

POWER MOVE

Check one credit-related account or report.

Write down:
- One positive habit you're already practicing
- One area you can improve

Focus on progress, not perfection.

JOURNAL

What emotions come up for me when I think about credit?

How has my past experience with credit influenced my current habits?

What would it look like to approach credit with intention instead of fear?

_____

_____

_____

_____

_____

_____

_____

_____

_____

CHAPTER 11
SAVING FOR KIDS: BUILDING GENERATIONAL STABILITY

Saving for children often feels overwhelming because it carries emotional weight.

Many parents want to give their children more opportunities than they had, but aren't always sure where to start or how much is "enough." The truth is, saving for kids isn't about perfection — it's about intention.

What Saving for Kids Really Means

Saving for kids doesn't have to look the same for everyone.
It's not about comparison or keeping up with what others are doing.

Saving for kids can mean:
- Preparing for education
- Creating financial stability
- Reducing future stress
- Teaching healthy money habits

Every small step contributes to long-term impact.

Different Ways to Save

There are multiple ways to save for children, and the right option depends on your goals, resources, and season of life.

Some common approaches include:
- Education-focused savings
- Custodial accounts
- Dedicated savings funds for future needs
- Savings bonds

What matters most is consistency, not complexity.

REAL TALK

For a long time, I felt pressure around saving for kids because I thought I needed to have everything figured out immediately. I compared myself to others and questioned whether I was doing enough.

What I learned was that saving for kids isn't about having a perfect plan — it's about making intentional choices when you can. Even small contributions created momentum and reduced stress over time.

Once I stopped comparing and started focusing on what made sense for my family, saving felt more manageable and less overwhelming.

Building stability didn't require huge amounts of money.
It required consistency and intention.

POWER MOVE

Decide what saving for your child looks like in this season.

Write down:
- The purpose of the savings
- The type of account or fund you want to use
- One small contribution you can start with

Focus on progress, not comparison.

JOURNAL

What does saving for my child or children mean to me personally?

What pressures or expectations have influenced how I think about saving for kids?

What small, intentional step could I take to support their future?

_____

_____

_____

_____

_____

_____

_____

_____

_____

_____

CHAPTER 12

BIG GOALS: SAVING FOR HOMES, CARS, VACATIONS, AND MORE

Big financial goals can feel intimidating when you look at them all at once.

Buying a home, purchasing a car, or planning a major vacation often feels out of reach, not because it's impossible, but because there's no clear plan in place. Big goals become manageable when they're broken down into smaller, intentional steps.

Why Big Goals Need Structure

Without structure, big goals stay in the "someday" category.
Structure turns dreams into plans.

When you define a goal clearly and give it a timeline, saving becomes purposeful instead of overwhelming. You're no longer guessing — you're preparing.

Approaching Big Purchases Intentionally

Big goals require more than hope.
They require clarity.

Intentional planning includes:
- Defining the total amount needed
- Setting a realistic timeline
- Saving consistently over time

Progress happens when the goal is specific and the plan is realistic.

REAL TALK

For a long time, big goals felt unrealistic to me.
Things like homeownership or buying a new car seemed like something other people did — not something that applied to my life.

What changed was learning how to plan instead of just wishing.
Once I broke big goals into smaller steps, they stopped feeling impossible.

Becoming a homeowner at 35 was a turning point for me.
It didn't happen overnight, and it wasn't luck.
It happened because I created systems, planned intentionally, and stayed consistent over time.

Big goals became achievable once I stopped seeing them as overwhelming and started seeing them as something I could prepare for.

POWER MOVE

Choose one financial account today and review it carefully.

Check for:
- Recent transactions
- Subscriptions or recurring charges
- Security settings and alerts

Write down one adjustment you can make to better protect your money.

JOURNAL

What big financial goals feel out of reach right now?

What beliefs or fears have made those goals feel unrealistic?

How would breaking one big goal into smaller steps change how I approach it?

_____

_____

_____

_____

_____

_____

_____

_____

_____

_____

_____

CHAPTER 13

STARTING A BUSINESS OR SIDE HUSTLE: YOUR FIRST STEPS TO EARNING MORE

Your First Steps to Earning More

Starting a business or side hustle often feels intimidating because people assume it requires a large investment, a perfect plan, or special credentials.

In reality, many successful income streams begin small and grow over time. The first step is not perfection — it's willingness.

What a Side Hustle Really Is

A side hustle doesn't have to be complicated.
It's simply a way to earn additional income using skills, knowledge, or resources you already have.

A side hustle can:
- Supplement your income
- Create flexibility
- Open doors to new opportunities
- Grow into something larger over time

Not every side hustle needs to become a full-time business.

Starting Where You Are

One of the biggest mistakes people make is waiting until everything feels ready. Clarity comes through action, not before it.

Starting small allows you to:
- Learn without overwhelming pressure
- Adjust as you go
- Build confidence through experience
- Reduce financial risk

REAL TALK

When I first started exploring additional income, I thought I needed everything figured out before I began. I believed I needed the perfect idea, the perfect plan, and the perfect timing.

What I learned instead was that progress came from trying. Some ideas worked. Others didn't. But every attempt taught me something valuable.

Starting small allowed me to learn without fear of failure. Over time, those small steps turned into real income streams and opportunities I couldn't have planned in advance.

I didn't need perfection.

I needed momentum.

POWER MOVE

Identify one idea you've been considering.

Write down:
- The problem it could solve
- Who it could help
- One small action you can take to explore it

Focus on learning, not perfection.

JOURNAL

Pick one idea and take action within 7 days - waiting to feel 'ready' costs you income.

Write the action down and the steps you will take to ensure you complete it within 7 days!

_____

_____

_____

_____

_____

_____

_____

_____

_____

CHAPTER 14
CONSISTENCY AND CONFIDENCE STAYING IN YOUR FINANCIAL LANE

Making more money is only part of the equation.

If your financial growth requires constant exhaustion, stress, or burnout, it isn't sustainable. True financial progress supports your life — it doesn't consume it.

Why Hustle Isn't the Goal

Hustle culture often celebrates doing more, working longer, and sacrificing rest. But burnout doesn't build wealth — it drains it.

Sustainable money habits are built on:
- Consistency over intensity
- Systems over willpower
- Balance over burnout

The goal is longevity, not constant grind.

Designing a Life-Supportive Financial Plan

A sustainable financial plan works with your life, not against it.

This includes:
- Income streams that fit your capacity
- Systems that reduce decision fatigue
- Financial goals that align with your priorities
- Space for rest, joy, and flexibility

Money should support the life you want to live.

REAL TALK

There was a time when I believed working harder was the answer to everything.
If something wasn't working financially, my solution was always to do more.

What I learned over time was that exhaustion isn't a strategy.
Burnout didn't bring clarity or stability — it created stress and inconsistency.

Once I focused on building systems instead of overworking myself, things changed.
My finances became more predictable, my stress decreased, and I had more control over my time.

Money started working for my life instead of running it.

POWER MOVE

Review one area of your finances that feels exhausting.

Write down:
- What makes it stressful
- What system could simplify it
- One small change you can make this month

Choose sustainability over burnout.

JOURNAL

Where do I feel pressure to overwork or overextend myself financially?

What would a more sustainable approach to money look like for my life?

Which areas of my finances could benefit from better systems instead of more effort?

_____

_____

_____

_____

_____

_____

_____

_____

_____

_____

CHAPTER 15
WORKSHEETS, CHECKLISTS, AND CHALLENGES: PUTTING IT ALL INTO PRACTICE

Money management isn't about mastering one tool.

It's about creating a system that works together.

Savings, budgeting, credit, income, and protection all support each other.
When these pieces are connected, your money becomes more predictable and easier to manage.

Why Systems Matter More Than Motivation

Motivation comes and goes.

Systems stay.

When your finances rely on willpower alone, progress is inconsistent.
Systems reduce decision-making, minimize stress, and keep things moving even when life gets busy.

Your System Will Look Different Than Anyone Else's

There is no one-size-fits-all money system.

Your system should reflect:
- Your income
- Your responsibilities
- Your goals
- Your capacity

What matters most is that your system supports your real life.

Introducing the Easiest System Ever: The 50 / 30 / 20 Plan

This is the system I personally love and use.

Why?

Because it's simple.
Because it's flexible.
And because it works for real people with real lives — not just spreadsheet gurus.

Here's How It Breaks Down:

- 50% Needs: These are your non-negotiables

- 30% Wants: These are the "nice to have" things that make life feel good

- 20% Savings: This is where the magic happens

50% Needs	30% Wants	20% Savings
Rent or mortgage	Eating out	Emergency fund
Utilities	Vacations	High-yield savings
Groceries	Grooming/Self-Care	Sinking funds
Transportation	Subscriptions	Extra debt payments
Insurance	Entertainment	Retirement
Minimum debt payments	Gifts	Investing
Child-related expenses	Hobbies	
Internet and phone	Shopping	

I want to be clear — I am not an affiliate of any high-yield bank, app, or tool mentioned in this book. I don't earn a penny if you open an account anywhere. I am simply sharing what has worked for me and what customers have had success with.
This is real-life advice, not sponsored content.

But What If Your Numbers Don't Fit 50/30/20?

Then you adjust them.

This is a guideline — not a rule.

If your rent is high, you might move wants to 25% and savings to 15%.

If you have kids, your needs may sit closer to 60%.

If you're aggressively saving for a home, your savings may move closer to 30%.

Make sure your spending has a purpose — even if that purpose changes month to month.

Your budget is allowed to be flexible.

- Life changes.
- Income changes.
- Priorities change.

Your budget should grow with you.

REAL TALK

What changed everything for me was realizing that no single strategy worked on its own.

- Saving without a plan felt frustrating.
- Budgeting without flexibility felt restrictive.
- Income without structure felt unstable.

Once I started connecting the pieces, things felt different.
My finances became more organized, less stressful, and easier to manage.

I didn't need more motivation.

I needed a system I could trust.

Building my personal money system gave me confidence because I knew what my money was doing — even when I wasn't thinking about it every day.

POWER MOVE

Sketch out your personal money system.

Write down:
- How money comes in
- Where it goes
- How it's protected
- How it supports your goals

You don't need perfection — just clarity.

JOURNAL

Which parts of my money system feel strong right now?

Which areas still feel disconnected or unclear?

What would it look like if my finances worked together instead of separately?

_____

_____

_____

_____

_____

_____

_____

_____

_____

_____

_____

REAL-LIFE MONEY CALLOUTS
Putting the Lessons Into Practice

$ ### Chapter 1 — Your Money Story
Understanding where you come from financially helps explain habits, beliefs, and patterns you may not even realize you have. Awareness is the first step to change.

$ ### Chapter 1A — Mindset Over Salary
Income alone doesn't create stability. Shifting how you think about money is what allows income to work for you instead of disappearing.

$ ### Chapter 2 — Taking Inventory
Looking at all accounts at once revealed patterns, habits, and opportunities for improvement that weren't visible when things were ignored or spread out.

$ ### Chapter 3 — Automations
Traditional savings accounts often pay as little as 0.01%, which is why automating transfers into high-yield savings accounts helped money grow more consistently without relying on memory or motivation.

$ ### Chapter 4 — Saving Challenges
Saving smaller, consistent amounts proved more effective than trying to save large sums sporadically. Habit mattered more than the method.

$ ### Chapter 5 — Protecting Your Money
Simple actions like adding beneficiaries, reviewing accounts regularly, and eliminating forgotten subscriptions helped prevent money from quietly leaking away.

$ ### Chapter 6 — Multiple Streams of Income
Additional income didn't start with a perfect plan. It started by using existing skills, focusing on one stream at a time, and allowing growth to happen gradually.

REAL-LIFE MONEY CALLOUTS
Putting the Lessons Into Practice

$ ### Chapter 7 — Budgeting
Simplifying budget categories made money management realistic and sustainable, removing the pressure of tracking every dollar perfectly.

$ ### Chapter 8 — Emergency Funds
Building an emergency fund — even in small amounts — created peace of mind and reduced the need to rely on credit during unexpected situations.

$ ### Chapter 9 — Sinking Funds
Planning ahead for known expenses like travel, holidays, and car maintenance prevented predictable costs from becoming financial emergencies.

$ ### Chapter 10 — Credit
Learning how credit actually works made it easier to manage balances, monitor accounts, and use credit intentionally instead of fearfully.

$ ### Chapter 11 — Saving for Kids
Saving for children became manageable by focusing on consistency and intention rather than comparison or unrealistic expectations.

$ ### Chapter 12 — Big Goals
Becoming a homeowner at 35 was the result of intentional planning, systems, and consistency — not luck or sudden income changes.

$ ### Chapter 13 — Side Hustles
Trying ideas, learning through experience, and starting small created real income opportunities without the pressure of perfection.

$ ### Chapter 14 — Sustainability
Shifting from overworking to building systems reduced stress and allowed money to support life instead of consuming it.

$ ### Chapter 15 — Personal Money Systems
Connecting savings, budgeting, income, credit, and protection into one system created clarity, confidence, and long-term stability.

NOTE PAGES JUST FOR YOU!

NOTE PAGES JUST FOR YOU! $

NOTE PAGES JUST FOR YOU!

NOTE PAGES JUST FOR YOU! $

NOTE PAGES JUST FOR YOU!

NOTE PAGES JUST FOR YOU! $

NOTE PAGES JUST FOR YOU!

NOTE PAGES JUST FOR YOU! $

NOTE PAGES JUST FOR YOU!

Hi Friend!

If there's one thing I hope you take from this book, it's this:

You don't have to be perfect with money to be powerful with it.

I didn't wake up one day with everything figured out.
I didn't grow up learning how money worked.
And I didn't build stability overnight.

What I did learn — step by step, mistake by mistake — is that progress comes from awareness, intention, and systems that support your real life.

This book isn't about doing everything at once.
It's about doing something — consistently.

You don't need a financial background.
You don't need a perfect plan.
You don't need to compare your journey to anyone else's.

You just need to start where you are and stay willing to learn.

From paycheck to power isn't a moment.
It's a process.

And if you're reading this, you're already in it!

- LaToya Hunter